Drop Shipping on eBay: A Beginner's Guide in 2024

Emy Diamondz

1

Copyright

The content contained in this book may not be reproduced, duplicated or transmitted without direct written permission from the author or the publisher.

Under no circumstances will any blame or legal responsibility be held against the publisher or author, for any damages, reparation or monetary loss due to the information contained within this book, either directly or indirectly.

Table of Contents

Introduction

Chapter 1: Introduction to Drop Shipping

Chapter 2: Getting Started with eBay Drop Shipping

Chapter 3: Finding Suppliers and Products

Chapter 4: Managing Orders and Customer Service

Chapter 5: Optimizing and Scaling Your eBay Drop Shipping Business

Introduction

Welcome to the world of eBay drop shipping for beginners in 2024! In today's digital age, e-commerce presents unparalleled opportunities for aspiring entrepreneurs to build successful online businesses with minimal upfront investment. Drop shipping, in particular, has emerged as a popular business model, allowing individuals to sell products to customers without the need to hold inventory or manage fulfillment.

In this comprehensive guide, we will embark on a journey to explore the fundamentals of drop shipping on eBay, providing beginners with the knowledge, strategies, and resources needed to kickstart their entrepreneurial endeavors and thrive in the competitive e-commerce landscape.

We will begin by defining drop shipping and understanding its benefits, particularly within the context of eBay as a leading online marketplace. From there, we will delve into the practical steps of setting up an eBay account, navigating policies, and conducting product research to identify profitable niches and products to sell.

Next, we will explore the process of finding reliable suppliers, evaluating product quality, and utilizing tools and platforms for effective product sourcing. With a solid understanding of sourcing strategies, we will then transition into managing orders and providing exceptional customer service, highlighting the importance of efficiency, communication, and customer satisfaction in driving business success.

As we progress, we will discuss strategies for optimizing and scaling your eBay drop shipping business, from refining operations and expanding product offerings to enhancing marketing efforts and fostering long-term growth. Throughout this journey, we will equip you with practical insights, actionable tips, and best practices to help you navigate the complexities of drop shipping on eBay and build a thriving online business.

Whether you're a seasoned entrepreneur looking to explore new opportunities or a beginner eager to dive into the world of e-commerce, this guide is designed to empower you with the knowledge and tools needed to succeed in eBay drop shipping in 2024 and beyond.

Chapter 1: Introduction to Drop Shipping

In this chapter, we delve into the fundamentals of drop shipping, providing beginners with a comprehensive understanding of the concept. We explore the definition of drop shipping, its advantages, and the reasons why eBay is a prime platform for drop shipping in 2024. By the end of this chapter, readers will have a solid foundation in drop shipping principles and its relevance to eBay.

What is Drop Shipping?

Drop shipping is a retail fulfillment method where a store doesn't keep the products it sells in stock. Instead, when a store sells a product, it purchases the item from a third party and has it shipped directly to the customer. In essence, the seller acts as a middleman, facilitating the transaction between the customer and the supplier without ever handling the product physically.

At its core, drop shipping involves three primary entities:

1. Retailer or Seller: This is the individual or business entity that markets and sells the products to customers. They create an online

storefront, whether it's through their website, an e-commerce platform like eBay, or other online marketplaces.

2. Supplier or Drop Shipper: The supplier is the entity that manufactures or warehouses the products. They maintain inventory and fulfill orders on behalf of the retailer. In a drop shipping arrangement, the retailer partners with the supplier to access their product catalog and fulfill customer orders.

3. Customer: The end consumer who purchases the product from the retailer. They place orders through the retailer's website or platform, and the retailer, in turn, coordinates with the supplier to fulfill those orders.

The drop shipping process typically unfolds as follows:

1. Product Selection: The retailer selects products from the supplier's catalog to list on their online store. These products can range from electronics

and clothing to household items and beyond.

2. Product Marketing and Sales: Once the products are listed, the retailer markets them to potential customers through various channels such as social media, search engine optimization (SEO), paid advertising, and email marketing. When a customer makes a purchase, the retailer collects payment from the customer.

3. Order Placement: Upon receiving an order from a customer, the retailer

forwards the order details (including the customer's shipping address) to the supplier.

4. Order Fulfillment: The supplier then processes the order, packages the product, and ships it directly to the customer. The retailer never handles the product physically, as it is shipped directly from the supplier to the customer.

5. Customer Service: Throughout the process, the retailer is responsible for providing customer support, including

handling inquiries, resolving issues, and managing returns or exchanges.

Drop shipping offers several advantages for both retailers and suppliers:

- Low Overhead Costs: Since retailers don't need to invest in inventory storage or manage fulfillment operations, they can start a business with minimal upfront costs.
- Wide Product Selection: Retailers have access to a vast array of products from multiple suppliers, allowing

them to offer a diverse product catalog without the need for warehousing.

- Location Independence: Drop shipping enables retailers to operate their businesses from anywhere with an internet connection, making it ideal for digital nomads or individuals looking for flexible work arrangements.

- Scalability: As retailers grow their businesses, they can easily scale up by adding new products or suppliers without the logistical challenges associated with traditional retail.

However, drop shipping also comes with its challenges and considerations, including:

- Thin Profit Margins: Since retailers typically purchase products at wholesale prices and sell them at retail prices, profit margins can be slim, especially when competing in saturated markets.

- Supplier Dependence: Retailers rely heavily on their suppliers for product quality, inventory availability, and order fulfillment. Issues with suppliers can directly impact the retailer's reputation and bottom line.

- Customer Service Management:
  Providing excellent customer service is
  essential for retaining customers and
  building a loyal customer base.
  Retailers must effectively manage
  customer inquiries, complaints, and
  returns to maintain customer
  satisfaction.

Overall, drop shipping presents a compelling opportunity for aspiring entrepreneurs to start an e-commerce business with minimal risk and investment. By understanding the intricacies of drop shipping and implementing sound business practices, retailers can build successful online ventures in today's competitive marketplace.

Benefits of Drop Shipping on eBay

Drop shipping on eBay offers a range of benefits for entrepreneurs looking to start or expand their e-commerce businesses. These advantages make it an attractive option for beginners and seasoned sellers alike. Here's a detailed look at the benefits of drop shipping on eBay:

1. Low Startup Costs: One of the most significant advantages of drop shipping on eBay is the low barrier to

entry. Unlike traditional retail models that require substantial upfront investment in inventory and storage space, drop shipping allows sellers to start with minimal capital. Since sellers only purchase products from suppliers after they've made a sale, there's no need to tie up funds in inventory.

2. No Inventory Management: With drop shipping, sellers don't need to worry about storing, managing, or shipping inventory. This eliminates the need for warehouse space, inventory tracking

systems, and fulfillment operations. Instead, sellers can focus on other aspects of their businesses, such as marketing, customer service, and business growth.

3. Wide Product Selection: Drop shipping enables sellers to offer a diverse range of products without the limitations of physical inventory. By partnering with multiple suppliers, sellers can access a vast catalog of products spanning various categories and niches. This allows them to cater to different customer preferences and

market demands, enhancing their competitiveness on eBay.

4. Flexibility and Scalability: Drop shipping offers sellers unparalleled flexibility and scalability. Since they don't need to pre-purchase inventory or manage fulfillment logistics, sellers can quickly adapt to changes in demand and market trends. Additionally, as their businesses grow, sellers can easily scale up by adding new products, suppliers, or sales channels without the constraints of traditional retail models.

5. Location Independence: Another advantage of drop shipping on eBay is the ability to operate a business from anywhere with an internet connection. Sellers are not tied to a specific location or physical storefront, allowing them to work remotely and pursue a flexible lifestyle. This makes drop shipping an attractive option for digital nomads, travelers, and individuals seeking work-from-home opportunities.

6. Reduced Risk and Overhead: Since sellers only purchase products from

suppliers after they've secured sales from customers, drop shipping minimizes the risk of overstocking or unsold inventory. This helps mitigate financial risks associated with traditional retail models, such as inventory depreciation, obsolescence, and storage costs. Additionally, sellers can test new products and markets with lower risk, allowing for experimentation and innovation in their businesses.

7. Access to eBay's Massive Customer Base: eBay boasts a vast and diverse

customer base, with millions of active buyers worldwide. By leveraging eBay's platform, drop shipping sellers can tap into this extensive network of potential customers, increasing their visibility and sales opportunities. eBay's robust search and recommendation algorithms further facilitate product discovery, helping sellers reach targeted audiences and drive traffic to their listings.

8. Built-in Trust and Credibility: eBay's reputation as a trusted online marketplace can benefit drop shipping

sellers by instilling confidence and trust in potential buyers. Many customers are familiar with eBay's buyer protection policies, secure payment methods, and feedback system, which can help alleviate concerns about purchasing from unfamiliar sellers. By operating within eBay's ecosystem, drop shipping sellers can leverage the platform's built-in trust and credibility to attract and retain customers.

Overall, drop shipping on eBay offers a compelling opportunity for entrepreneurs to build successful e-commerce businesses with minimal risk and investment. By harnessing the benefits of drop shipping and leveraging eBay's platform, sellers can access a global marketplace, offer a wide range of products, and achieve sustainable growth in today's competitive e-commerce landscape.

Why Choose eBay for Drop Shipping in 2024?

Choosing eBay as a platform for drop shipping in 2024 offers several distinct advantages for entrepreneurs looking to establish or expand their e-commerce businesses. While there are various online marketplaces available, eBay continues to stand out as a preferred choice for drop shipping for the following reasons:

1. Established Reputation and Trust: eBay is one of the oldest and most well-established online marketplaces, with a proven track record of connecting buyers and sellers worldwide. Over the years, eBay has built a strong reputation for reliability, security, and buyer protection, which instills trust and confidence among

customers. For drop shipping sellers, leveraging eBay's trusted platform can help overcome buyer skepticism and encourage sales.

2. Massive Customer Base: With millions of active buyers visiting the platform daily, eBay offers drop shipping sellers access to a vast and diverse customer base. This extensive reach increases the visibility of sellers' listings and expands their sales opportunities. By tapping into eBay's large audience, drop shipping sellers can attract potential customers from around the

globe, driving traffic and generating revenue.

3. Robust Search and Recommendation Algorithms: eBay's sophisticated search and recommendation algorithms make it easier for buyers to discover products that match their preferences and interests. By optimizing product listings with relevant keywords, high-quality images, and detailed descriptions, drop shipping sellers can improve their visibility in eBay search results and increase their chances of reaching

targeted audiences. eBay's
recommendation engine also suggests
relevant products to users based on
their browsing and purchase history,
helping sellers boost sales through
personalized recommendations.

4. Seller-Friendly Policies and Tools:
eBay offers a range of seller-friendly
policies and tools designed to support
entrepreneurs and enhance their
selling experience. These include seller
protection programs, streamlined
listing tools, promotional tools, and
analytics dashboards. Additionally,

eBay provides educational resources, tutorials, and customer support to help sellers navigate the platform effectively and maximize their success. By leveraging eBay's seller-centric ecosystem, drop shipping sellers can streamline their operations, mitigate risks, and optimize their sales strategies.

5. Flexible Listing Options: eBay offers flexible listing options that cater to different types of products and selling strategies. Whether sellers prefer auction-style listings, fixed-price

listings, or a combination of both, eBay provides the flexibility to accommodate their preferences. This versatility allows drop shipping sellers to experiment with different pricing strategies, listing formats, and promotional tactics to optimize their sales and maximize profitability.

6. International Selling Opportunities: eBay's global marketplace enables drop shipping sellers to reach customers in multiple countries and regions worldwide. With localized versions of the platform available in

various languages and currencies, sellers can easily expand their reach beyond their domestic markets and tap into lucrative international markets. eBay also offers tools and resources to facilitate cross-border trade, including international shipping options, customs documentation assistance, and localized customer support.

7. Adaptability to Market Trends: eBay's dynamic marketplace adapts to evolving consumer preferences, market trends, and industry shifts. By

staying attuned to market dynamics and consumer behavior, drop shipping sellers can capitalize on emerging trends, seasonal demand fluctuations, and niche opportunities. eBay's agile platform allows sellers to quickly adjust their product offerings, pricing strategies, and marketing campaigns to stay competitive and maximize sales in a rapidly changing e-commerce landscape.

In conclusion, eBay remains a compelling choice for drop shipping in 2024 due to its established reputation, massive customer base, robust infrastructure, seller-friendly policies, flexible listing options, international selling opportunities, and adaptability to market trends. By harnessing the power of eBay's platform, drop shipping sellers can build successful e-commerce businesses, drive growth, and achieve sustainable success in today's competitive online marketplace.

Chapter 2: Getting Started with eBay Drop Shipping

In this chapter, we provide a comprehensive guide for beginners looking to embark on their eBay drop shipping journey. From setting up an eBay account to understanding the platform's policies and guidelines, readers will gain the necessary knowledge and insights to kickstart their drop shipping business on eBay.

1. Setting Up Your eBay Account:
    - Creating a Seller Account: We walk readers through the process of setting up a seller

account on eBay, including
selecting a username, providing
contact information, and
verifying their identity.

- o Understanding Account Types:
  We explain the different types of
  eBay seller accounts, such as
  individual and business
  accounts, and help readers
  choose the most suitable option
  for their drop shipping venture.
- o Completing Account Setup: We
  guide readers through the
  remaining steps of account

setup, including linking payment methods, setting up shipping preferences, and configuring seller preferences.

2. Understanding eBay Policies and Guidelines:

   - eBay's Drop Shipping Policy: We provide an overview of eBay's drop shipping policy, including guidelines for drop shipping sellers and best practices to ensure compliance with eBay's rules and regulations.

o   Seller Performance Standards:
    We discuss eBay's seller
    performance standards and the
    importance of maintaining high
    levels of customer satisfaction,
    prompt shipping, and accurate
    item descriptions to avoid
    penalties and account
    restrictions.

o   Prohibited and Restricted Items:
    We outline eBay's policies
    regarding prohibited and
    restricted items, including
    products that cannot be sold on

the platform due to legal or safety concerns. We also advise readers on how to identify and avoid listing such items in their drop shipping inventory.

3. Researching Profitable Niches and Products:

   o Market Research Strategies: We introduce readers to market research techniques for identifying profitable niches and products on eBay. This includes analyzing market trends, competitor analysis, keyword research, and using eBay's own research tools.

- o Product Sourcing Methods: We explore various methods for sourcing products for drop shipping, including partnering with reputable suppliers, utilizing wholesale marketplaces, and leveraging drop shipping directories and platforms.

- o Evaluating Profitability: We teach readers how to assess the profitability of potential products by considering factors such as wholesale prices, shipping costs, eBay fees, and estimated selling prices. We also provide tips for calculating profit margins and setting competitive prices to maximize earnings.

By the end of this chapter, readers will have a solid understanding of the essential steps and considerations involved in getting started with eBay drop shipping. Armed with this knowledge, they will be well-equipped to launch their drop shipping business on eBay and navigate the platform's policies and guidelines effectively.

Implementing Effective Marketing Strategies

In this section, we explore various marketing strategies tailored specifically for eBay drop shipping sellers to maximize visibility, attract customers, and drive sales.

1. Optimized Product Listings:
    - Title Optimization: Crafting compelling and keyword-rich titles that accurately describe the product and include relevant

keywords to improve search
visibility.

- Detailed Descriptions: Providing
  detailed and informative
  product descriptions that
  highlight key features,
  specifications, and benefits to
  help customers make informed
  purchasing decisions.

- High-Quality Images: Using
  high-resolution images that
  showcase the product from
  multiple angles and provide

clear visuals of its appearance, quality, and functionality.

- o Utilizing Item Specifics: Completing item specifics fields with relevant details such as brand, size, color, and condition to enhance searchability and filter options for buyers.

2. Search Engine Optimization (SEO):

- o Keyword Research: Conducting keyword research to identify relevant and high-volume search terms related to the products being sold and incorporating

them strategically into product
listings and descriptions.

- Optimized Storefront:
  Optimizing the eBay seller
  storefront with relevant
  keywords, categories, and
  descriptions to improve search
  engine rankings and attract
  organic traffic.

- Backlink Building: Building
  backlinks from external sources
  such as blogs, forums, and social
  media platforms to increase the
  authority and visibility of eBay

listings in search engine results
pages (SERPs).

3. Paid Advertising:

   o Promoted Listings: Utilizing
   eBay's Promoted Listings feature
   to boost the visibility of select
   products by paying a fee to have
   them featured prominently in
   search results and on relevant
   category pages.

   o Google Shopping Campaigns:
   Creating Google Shopping
   campaigns to showcase eBay
   listings on Google's search

engine results and Shopping tab, reaching potential customers who are actively searching for products online.

- Social Media Ads: Running targeted advertising campaigns on popular social media platforms such as Facebook, Instagram, and Pinterest to reach specific demographics and drive traffic to eBay listings.

4. Email Marketing:

- Customer Segmentation: Segmenting email lists based on

customer preferences, purchase history, and behavior to personalize marketing messages and promotions for different audience segments.

- Automated Campaigns: Setting up automated email campaigns for welcome messages, abandoned cart reminders, product recommendations, and special promotions to engage customers and encourage repeat purchases.

- Newsletter Subscriptions:
    Offering incentives such as
    discounts or exclusive offers to
    encourage customers to
    subscribe to email newsletters,
    enabling regular communication
    and updates on new products
    and promotions.

5. Customer Reviews and Feedback:

   - Encouraging Positive Reviews:
     Providing excellent customer
     service and timely order
     fulfillment to encourage positive
     reviews and ratings from

satisfied customers, which can
enhance credibility and
trustworthiness.

- Responding to Feedback:
  Actively monitoring and
  responding to customer
  feedback, whether positive or
  negative, to address concerns,
  resolve issues, and demonstrate
  responsiveness and commitment
  to customer satisfaction.
- Leveraging Social Proof:
  Showcasing positive reviews,
  testimonials, and customer

testimonials on product listings and the seller storefront to build social proof and reassure potential buyers of the quality and reliability of products and services.

By implementing these effective marketing strategies, eBay drop shipping sellers can increase visibility, attract targeted traffic, and drive conversions, ultimately maximizing sales and profitability on the platform.

Monitoring Performance Metrics and Analytics

In this section, we delve into the importance of tracking performance metrics and utilizing analytics tools to assess the effectiveness of eBay drop shipping strategies and optimize business operations.

1. Key Performance Indicators (KPIs):

    o Sales Metrics: Tracking sales performance metrics such as total sales volume, revenue, average order value (AOV), and conversion rates to gauge overall business performance and identify trends over time.

- Traffic Sources: Analyzing traffic sources and referral sources to understand where website visitors are coming from, which marketing channels are driving the most traffic, and which sources are converting the highest.

- Customer Behavior: Monitoring customer behavior metrics such as bounce rate, time on site, pages per visit, and repeat purchase rate to evaluate user engagement, satisfaction, and loyalty.

- o Inventory Management: Tracking inventory turnover rate, stock levels, and out-of-stock occurrences to optimize inventory management processes, prevent stockouts, and ensure timely order fulfillment.

2. eBay Seller Dashboard:

- o eBay Analytics: Leveraging eBay's built-in analytics tools and seller dashboard to access real-time data and insights on sales performance, traffic metrics, listing impressions, and seller performance metrics.

- Performance Reports: Generating and analyzing performance reports provided by eBay to track sales trends, monitor seller performance metrics, and identify areas for improvement or optimization.

3. Third-Party Analytics Tools:

    o   Google Analytics: Integrating
        Google Analytics with eBay
        storefronts to track website
        traffic, user behavior, and
        conversion metrics, allowing for
        more in-depth analysis and
        customization of tracking
        parameters.

    o   Data Analysis Platforms: Using
        third-party data analysis
        platforms such as Tableau,
        Microsoft Power BI, or Data
        Studio to aggregate and visualize

data from multiple sources,
enabling advanced analytics and
insights generation.

4. A/B Testing:

   - Testing Variations: Conducting
     A/B tests to compare different
     variations of product listings,
     marketing campaigns, pricing
     strategies, and website design
     elements to determine which
     variations perform best in terms
     of sales, conversions, and
     customer engagement.

- Data-driven Decision Making:
  Using A/B testing results to
  inform data-driven decision
  making and optimize strategies
  for maximizing sales, improving
  customer experience, and
  driving business growth.

5. Continuous Optimization:

   - Iterative Improvement:
     Continuously analyzing
     performance metrics and testing
     different strategies, tactics, and
     optimizations to identify
     opportunities for improvement

and refine business processes over time.

- ○ Responsive Strategy Adjustments: Adapting marketing strategies, pricing strategies, product offerings, and operational processes based on performance data and feedback to align with changing market conditions and customer preferences.

By actively monitoring performance metrics and leveraging analytics tools, eBay drop shipping sellers can gain valuable insights into their businesses' performance, identify areas for optimization, and make data-driven decisions to drive growth, enhance profitability, and achieve long-term success on the platform.

Scaling Your Business for Long-Term Success

Scaling a drop shipping business on eBay involves strategically expanding operations, increasing sales volume, and optimizing processes to sustain growth and profitability over the long term. In this section, we outline key strategies for scaling a eBay drop shipping business effectively:

1. Expand Product Catalog:

   o Diversify Product Range:
     Continuously expand the
     product catalog by adding new
     and complementary products to
     attract a broader audience and
     cater to different customer
     preferences and needs.

   o Trend Analysis: Monitor market
     trends, consumer demand, and
     competitor offerings to identify
     emerging trends and capitalize
     on new opportunities for
     product expansion.

o   Seasonal Offerings: Introduce seasonal products and limited-time promotions to capitalize on seasonal demand fluctuations and drive incremental sales during peak seasons.

2. Optimize Supplier Relationships:

o   Establish Partnerships: Cultivate strong relationships with reliable suppliers and wholesalers to access a broader range of products, negotiate favorable pricing terms, and ensure consistent product quality and availability.

- Negotiate Volume Discounts: Negotiate volume discounts and bulk pricing agreements with suppliers to reduce costs and improve profit margins as sales volume increases.

- Streamline Order Fulfillment: Work closely with suppliers to streamline order fulfillment processes, optimize shipping times, and minimize delays to ensure timely delivery and enhance customer satisfaction.

3. Invest in Marketing and Advertising:

    o   Scale Advertising Efforts: Increase investments in paid advertising channels such as Google Ads, Facebook Ads, and promoted listings on eBay to expand reach, drive targeted traffic, and generate higher sales volume.

    o   Retargeting Campaigns: Implement retargeting campaigns to re-engage with previous website visitors and abandoned cart users, increasing conversion rates and maximizing sales opportunities.

- Content Marketing: Invest in content marketing initiatives such as blogging, email newsletters, and social media content to build brand awareness, foster customer engagement, and drive organic traffic to eBay listings.

4. Improve Operational Efficiency:

- o Automation Tools: Implement automation tools and software solutions to streamline repetitive tasks, such as order processing, inventory management, and customer support, freeing up time to focus on strategic growth initiatives.

- o Outsourcing Tasks: Consider outsourcing non-core functions such as customer service, order fulfillment, and administrative tasks to third-party service providers or virtual assistants to scale operations efficiently.

- Performance Monitoring: Continuously monitor key performance metrics and analytics to identify bottlenecks, inefficiencies, and areas for improvement in business processes and workflows.

5. Enhance Customer Experience:

- Provide Exceptional Service: Prioritize customer satisfaction by providing prompt, friendly, and personalized customer

service, resolving issues
promptly, and exceeding
customer expectations to foster
loyalty and encourage repeat
purchases.

o Offer Value-Added Services:
Differentiate your business by
offering value-added services
such as free shipping, extended
warranties, product
customization options, or loyalty
rewards programs to enhance
the overall customer experience
and drive customer retention.

- ○ Solicit Feedback: Actively solicit feedback from customers through surveys, reviews, and social media channels to gain insights into their preferences, pain points, and satisfaction levels, and use this feedback to continuously improve products and services.

By implementing these scalable strategies and continuously optimizing business operations, eBay drop shipping sellers can position themselves for long-term success, sustain growth, and thrive in a competitive e-commerce landscape.

Setting Up Your eBay Account

Setting up an eBay account is the first step for beginners looking to start their drop shipping journey on the platform. Follow these step-by-step instructions to create your eBay seller account:

1. Visit eBay's Website: Open your web browser and navigate to eBay's official website (www.ebay.com).

2. Click on "Register": On the eBay homepage, locate the "Register"

option at the top left corner of the
screen and click on it.

3. Choose Account Type: eBay offers two
   types of seller accounts: "Personal"
   and "Business." Select the option that
   best fits your needs and click
   "Continue."

4. Enter Personal Information: Fill out
   the registration form with your
   personal information, including your
   name, email address, and desired
   password. Make sure to choose a
   strong password to secure your
   account.

5. Verify Email Address: After completing the registration form, eBay will send a verification email to the email address you provided. Check your inbox and click on the verification link to confirm your email address.

6. Complete Verification: Follow the prompts to complete the verification process and confirm your identity. You may need to enter additional information or provide identification documents, depending on the account type and eBay's requirements.

7. Provide Payment Information: If you're setting up a business account or plan to sell items that require payment processing, such as electronics or high-value items, you'll need to provide payment information, such as a credit card or bank account details.

8. Set Up Seller Preferences: Once your account is verified, you'll be prompted to set up seller preferences, including shipping options, return policies, and payment methods. Review and configure these settings according to your business needs and preferences.

9. Confirm Account Creation: After completing the registration process and setting up your seller preferences, eBay will confirm the creation of your seller account. You'll receive a confirmation message or notification indicating that your eBay account is now active and ready for use.

10. Start Listing Products: With your eBay account set up, you can now start listing products for sale on the platform. Use eBay's listing tools to create detailed product listings with photos, descriptions, and pricing

information to attract potential buyers.

Congratulations! You've successfully set up your eBay seller account and are ready to begin your drop shipping journey on the platform. Remember to adhere to eBay's policies and guidelines, provide excellent customer service, and continuously optimize your listings to maximize sales and grow your business.

Understanding eBay Policies and Guidelines

Before starting your drop shipping business on eBay, it's crucial to familiarize yourself with eBay's policies and guidelines to ensure compliance and avoid potential issues. Here's a breakdown of key eBay policies and guidelines that every seller should understand:

1. Drop Shipping Policy:
   - eBay allows drop shipping, but sellers are responsible for ensuring a positive buying experience for customers.

- Sellers must have physical possession of the item(s) being sold and must be able to fulfill orders promptly.

  - Sellers should avoid using third-party suppliers or distributors who ship directly to customers without the seller ever physically handling the item.

2. Seller Performance Standards:

  - eBay has seller performance standards that sellers must meet to maintain a good standing on the platform.

- Performance metrics include feedback score, detailed seller ratings (DSRs), cases opened by buyers, and late shipments.
- Sellers who consistently fail to meet these standards may face penalties, such as lower search visibility, account restrictions, or suspension.

3. Prohibited and Restricted Items:

- eBay prohibits the sale of certain items due to legal or safety reasons, such as counterfeit goods, weapons, drugs, and hazardous materials.

- Some items may be restricted or require special approval before listing, such as alcohol, tobacco products, and certain electronics.

- Sellers should review eBay's list of prohibited and restricted items regularly to ensure compliance and avoid listing violations.

4. Listing Policies:

- eBay has specific listing policies that sellers must follow when creating product listings.

- Listings must accurately describe the item being sold, including its condition, specifications, and any defects or imperfections.

- Sellers should use clear and high-quality photos of the actual item, not stock images, to

represent the product
accurately.

- o Listings must comply with
  eBay's pricing policies, including
  avoiding misleading or inflated
  pricing practices.

5. Shipping and Returns:

- o Sellers are responsible for
  setting up shipping options,
  including shipping costs,
  delivery methods, and handling
  times.

- o eBay encourages sellers to offer free shipping or competitive shipping rates to attract buyers.
- o Sellers should have clear and reasonable return policies, including refund options, return periods, and conditions for returns.

6. Customer Service:

- o Providing excellent customer service is essential for maintaining buyer satisfaction and positive feedback.

- Sellers should respond promptly
  to buyer inquiries, address any
  issues or concerns, and resolve
  disputes professionally.

- eBay offers tools and resources
  to help sellers manage customer
  service effectively, such as eBay
  Messages and Resolution
  Center.

7. Intellectual Property Rights:

   - Sellers must respect intellectual
     property rights, including
     trademarks, copyrights, and
     patents.

- Listings should not infringe on the intellectual property of others, such as using copyrighted images or selling counterfeit goods.
  - eBay has processes in place for reporting and resolving intellectual property violations, including VeRO (Verified Rights Owner) program.

It's essential to review and understand eBay's policies and guidelines thoroughly before starting your drop shipping business on the platform. By adhering to these policies and providing a positive buying experience for customers, you can build a reputable and successful business on eBay.

Researching Profitable Niches and Products

Conducting thorough research to identify profitable niches and products is essential for success in drop shipping on eBay. Here's a step-by-step guide to researching profitable niches and products:

1. Market Analysis:
   - Identify Trends: Start by identifying current market

trends and consumer
preferences. Look for products
that are in high demand or
experiencing growth in
popularity.

- o Analyze Competition: Research
  competitors selling similar
  products on eBay. Analyze their
  pricing strategies, product
  offerings, customer reviews, and
  sales volume to identify gaps or
  opportunities in the market.
- o Explore Niche Markets:
  Consider exploring niche

markets or specialized product
categories with less competition
but strong demand. Look for
underserved or emerging niches
that present opportunities for
differentiation and growth.

2. Keyword Research:

   o Utilize eBay's Search Bar: Use
     eBay's search bar to identify
     popular search terms and
     keywords related to your
     potential niche or product
     category. Pay attention to

autocomplete suggestions and related search terms.

- Keyword Tools: Use keyword research tools such as Google Keyword Planner, SEMrush, or Ahrefs to identify relevant keywords with high search volume and low competition. Focus on long-tail keywords that are specific to your niche or product.

3. Product Demand and Profitability:

- Analyze Sales Data: Use eBay's advanced search filters and tools to analyze sales data for specific products or categories. Look for products with consistent sales volume, high sell-through rates, and stable pricing trends.

○ Calculate Profit Margins: Consider factors such as wholesale prices, shipping costs, eBay fees, and potential profit margins when evaluating product profitability. Look for products with healthy profit margins that align with your business goals.

4. Supplier Research:

   o   Identify Reliable Suppliers:
       Research and vet potential
       suppliers or wholesalers who
       offer products in your chosen
       niche. Look for suppliers with a
       reputation for reliability, quality
       products, and competitive
       pricing.

   o   Contact Suppliers: Reach out to
       potential suppliers to inquire
       about product availability,
       pricing, minimum order
       quantities, and shipping options.

Request samples to evaluate
product quality firsthand before
committing to a supplier.

5. Evaluate Market Demand:

    ○ Validate Demand: Validate
      market demand for your chosen
      niche or products by conducting
      surveys, polls, or market
      research studies. Engage with
      potential customers on social
      media platforms, forums, or
      online communities to gather
      insights and feedback.

o   Monitor Trends: Stay updated on industry trends, seasonal fluctuations, and consumer preferences to anticipate changes in demand and adapt your product offerings accordingly. Follow industry news, attend trade shows, and subscribe to relevant publications to stay informed.

6. Consider Profitable Niches:

o   Evergreen Products: Consider selling evergreen products with consistent demand year-round, such as electronics, home goods, or health and wellness products.

- Seasonal Products: Explore seasonal product categories that experience spikes in demand during specific times of the year, such as holiday decorations, outdoor gear, or back-to-school supplies.

- Trending Products: Keep an eye on trending products and emerging trends in popular culture, fashion, technology, and lifestyle categories.

- Capitalize on viral trends and
  fads to capitalize on short-term
  opportunities.

Chapter 3: Finding Suppliers and Products

In this chapter, we explore the crucial process of finding reliable suppliers and profitable products for your eBay drop shipping business. We'll cover various methods and strategies to identify reputable suppliers and source high-demand products to maximize your chances of success.

1. Identifying Reliable Suppliers:

   - Research Supplier Directories:
     Explore online supplier directories and platforms such as Alibaba, SaleHoo, or

Worldwide Brands to find
reputable suppliers in your
niche.

- o Attend Trade Shows: Attend
  industry trade shows and
  exhibitions to connect with
  potential suppliers, evaluate
  product samples, and establish
  relationships with
  manufacturers and wholesalers.
- o Network with Other Sellers: Join
  online forums, social media
  groups, or networking events to
  connect with other drop

shipping sellers and exchange
recommendations and insights
on reliable suppliers.

- Check Supplier Reviews: Look
  for reviews and testimonials
  from other sellers or buyers who
  have worked with the supplier
  before. Pay attention to factors
  such as product quality,
  communication, shipping times,
  and customer service.

- Request Samples: Request
  samples from potential suppliers
  to evaluate product quality

firsthand before committing to a partnership. Assess factors such as product durability, packaging, and overall satisfaction.

2. Evaluating Product Quality and Demand:

    o Analyze Market Trends: Use market research tools and analytics to identify trending products and high-demand niches. Look for products with consistent sales volume and positive growth trends.

- Conduct Keyword Research: Use keyword research tools to identify popular search terms and phrases related to your niche. Focus on long-tail keywords with high search volume and low competition to target specific customer needs and preferences.

- Review Competitor Offerings: Analyze competitor listings and pricing strategies to identify gaps or opportunities in the market. Look for underserved or niche product categories with less competition but strong demand.

- o Consider Profit Margins: Calculate potential profit margins for each product based on factors such as wholesale prices, shipping costs, eBay fees, and estimated selling prices. Choose products with healthy profit margins that align with your business goals and financial objectives.

- Monitor Seasonal Trends: Anticipate seasonal fluctuations in demand and adjust your product offerings accordingly. Consider offering seasonal products or promotions to capitalize on peak shopping seasons and maximize sales opportunities.

3. Utilizing Tools and Platforms:

   - eBay Wholesale Deals: Explore eBay's Wholesale Deals program to access discounted products and exclusive offers from

verified suppliers. Browse
through a curated selection of
products across various
categories and source inventory
directly from trusted suppliers.

- Drop Shipping Directories:
  Consider subscribing to drop
  shipping directories or platforms
  such as SaleHoo, Worldwide
  Brands, or Oberlo to access
  pre-vetted suppliers and curated
  product listings. These
  directories offer a convenient
  and reliable way to find

suppliers and source products
for your eBay business.

- Supplier Websites: Visit supplier
  websites directly to explore their
  product catalogs, pricing
  information, and ordering
  process. Many suppliers offer
  drop shipping services and
  provide resources and support
  for drop shipping sellers.

By following these strategies and utilizing
various resources, you can effectively find
reliable suppliers and source profitable
products to build a successful drop shipping

business on eBay. Continuously evaluate market trends, monitor product performance, and adapt your product selection to meet customer demand and maximize sales potential.

Identifying Reliable Suppliers

Finding reliable suppliers is essential for the success of your eBay drop shipping business. Here are some effective strategies to identify trustworthy suppliers:

1. Supplier Directories: Explore reputable supplier directories such as Alibaba, SaleHoo, and Worldwide

Brands. These directories provide a comprehensive list of verified suppliers across various industries and product categories. You can filter suppliers based on location, product type, and minimum order quantity (MOQ), making it easier to find suitable partners for your business.

2. Trade Shows and Exhibitions: Attend industry-specific trade shows, exhibitions, and conferences to connect with potential suppliers face-to-face. Trade shows offer a valuable opportunity to meet

suppliers, evaluate product samples, and establish personal relationships. Look for trade shows relevant to your niche and industry to find reputable suppliers.

3. Online Research: Conduct thorough online research to find suppliers that meet your criteria. Utilize search engines, online forums, and social media platforms to discover suppliers recommended by other sellers or industry experts. Look for suppliers with positive reviews, a strong online

presence, and a track record of reliability.

4. Networking: Network with other drop shipping sellers, industry professionals, and business owners to gather recommendations and referrals for reliable suppliers. Join online communities, forums, and social media groups where sellers share insights, tips, and recommendations for sourcing suppliers. Networking can help you discover hidden gems and access exclusive supplier contacts.

5. Certifications and Associations: Look for suppliers that are members of industry associations or hold relevant certifications and accreditations. Suppliers with certifications such as ISO 9001 or memberships in trade associations demonstrate a commitment to quality, professionalism, and ethical business practices. Check for certifications and affiliations on supplier websites or inquire directly with the supplier.

6. Supplier Reviews and References: Research supplier reviews and

testimonials from other sellers or buyers who have worked with the supplier before. Look for feedback on factors such as product quality, reliability, communication, and customer service. You can find reviews on supplier directories, forums, review websites, and social media platforms.

7. Communication and Transparency: Reach out to potential suppliers and communicate directly to assess their responsiveness, professionalism, and transparency. Ask questions about their products, services, pricing, and

policies to gauge their level of expertise and willingness to collaborate. Pay attention to how quickly and thoroughly they respond to your inquiries.

8. Sample Orders: Request samples from potential suppliers to evaluate product quality, packaging, and shipping times firsthand. Sampling allows you to assess the supplier's reliability and the suitability of their products for your business. Consider ordering samples from multiple suppliers to compare

quality and make an informed
decision.

By utilizing these strategies and conducting thorough due diligence, you can identify reliable suppliers for your eBay drop shipping business. Remember to prioritize quality, reliability, and transparency when selecting suppliers to ensure a successful and sustainable partnership.

Evaluating Product Quality and Pricing

When sourcing products for your eBay drop shipping business, it's essential to evaluate both the quality of the products and their pricing to ensure profitability and customer satisfaction. Here are some key factors to consider when evaluating product quality and pricing:

1. Product Quality:

    o Physical Inspection: If possible, request samples of the products from your suppliers to inspect their quality firsthand. Pay attention to details such as materials, construction, durability, and overall craftsmanship.

- ○ Customer Reviews: Research customer reviews and feedback for the products you're considering selling. Look for patterns in feedback regarding product quality, performance, and durability. Positive reviews indicate satisfied customers, while negative reviews may indicate potential issues with the product.

- ○ Return Rates: Analyze return rates for the products to gauge customer satisfaction and product quality. High return rates may indicate dissatisfaction with the product, poor quality, or inaccurate product descriptions.

- Brand Reputation: Consider the reputation of the brand or manufacturer behind the products. Established brands with a track record of producing high-quality products are generally a safer bet than lesser-known or generic brands.

2. Pricing:

   - Cost of Goods Sold (COGS):
     Calculate the cost of goods sold
     (COGS) for each product,
     including the wholesale price
     from your supplier, shipping
     costs, and any additional fees or
     expenses. Ensure that your
     selling price covers your COGS
     while still allowing for a
     reasonable profit margin.

- Competitive Analysis: Research competitors' prices for similar products to understand market pricing trends and competitive benchmarks. Compare your prices to those of competitors to ensure that they are competitive while still allowing for profitability.

- Price vs. Quality: Consider the relationship between price and quality when setting your prices. Higher-priced products may be perceived as higher quality, but

they also need to justify the price
with superior features,
materials, or craftsmanship.

- o Perceived Value: Assess the
  perceived value of the product to
  customers based on factors such
  as brand reputation, product
  features, and customer reviews.
  Customers are often willing to
  pay more for products that offer
  unique features, superior
  quality, or brand prestige.
- o Dynamic Pricing: Monitor
  market demand and adjust your

prices dynamically to remain competitive and maximize profitability. Use pricing strategies such as discounts, promotions, and bundling to attract customers and drive sales without sacrificing margins.

3. Profitability:

   o Gross Profit Margin: Calculate the gross profit margin for each product by subtracting the COGS from the selling price and dividing by the selling price. Aim for a healthy profit margin that covers your expenses and leaves room for reinvestment and growth.

- Volume Discounts: Negotiate volume discounts with your suppliers to lower your COGS and increase your profit margins. Bulk purchasing allows you to secure better pricing and improve your profitability over time.

- Shipping Costs: Factor shipping costs into your pricing strategy to ensure that they are covered

while remaining competitive.
Consider offering free shipping
or flat-rate shipping to simplify
pricing for customers and
increase conversion rates.

By carefully evaluating product quality and pricing, you can select high-quality products at competitive prices that appeal to customers and drive sales on eBay.

Utilizing Tools and Platforms for Product Sourcing

Finding reliable suppliers and sourcing profitable products is made easier with the help of various tools and platforms specifically designed for product sourcing. Here are some effective tools and platforms to aid in your product sourcing efforts for your eBay drop shipping business:

1. SaleHoo:

    o SaleHoo is a comprehensive directory of wholesalers, drop shippers, manufacturers, and

liquidators across various
product categories.

- o It provides access to over 8,000
  pre-vetted suppliers, making it
  easy to find reliable partners for
  your drop shipping business.
- o SaleHoo offers advanced search
  filters, supplier reviews, and
  market research tools to help
  you identify profitable products
  and suppliers.

2. Alibaba:

- o Alibaba is one of the largest
  online marketplaces for sourcing

products directly from
manufacturers and wholesalers
in China and other countries.

- It offers a vast selection of
  products across numerous
  categories, including electronics,
  fashion, home goods, and more.
- Alibaba provides tools such as
  product search, supplier
  verification, and trade assurance
  to ensure transparency and
  reliability in transactions.

3. Oberlo:

   - Oberlo is a drop shipping platform that integrates seamlessly with Shopify, allowing you to easily import products from suppliers and automate order fulfillment.

   - It offers a wide range of products sourced from AliExpress, making it convenient for Shopify store owners to find and add products to their stores.

- Oberlo's user-friendly interface and features, such as product customization and order tracking, streamline the drop shipping process for sellers.

4. Worldwide Brands:

   - Worldwide Brands is a wholesale directory featuring over 16 million products from thousands of certified suppliers and wholesalers.

   - It offers access to genuine wholesale suppliers and

products, ensuring quality and authenticity for sellers.

- o Worldwide Brands provides in-depth supplier research tools, market analysis, and educational resources to help sellers succeed in their drop shipping ventures.

5. Google Trends:

- o Google Trends is a free tool that allows you to track the popularity of search terms and topics over time.

- o Use Google Trends to identify trending products and niche

markets with growing demand,
helping you make informed
decisions about product
selection.

- Analyze search trends, regional
  interest, and related topics to
  discover opportunities for
  product sourcing and market
  expansion.

6. eBay Wholesale Deals:

   - eBay Wholesale Deals is a
     program that offers discounted
     wholesale products directly from
     verified suppliers on eBay.

- o It provides access to a curated selection of products across various categories, including electronics, fashion, home goods, and more.

- o eBay Wholesale Deals offers exclusive discounts and promotions for eBay sellers, making it a convenient option for sourcing inventory directly on the platform.

Chapter 4: Managing Orders and Customer Service

In this chapter, we delve into the essential aspects of effectively managing orders and providing exceptional customer service in your eBay drop shipping business. We'll cover strategies and best practices to streamline order fulfillment, handle customer inquiries, and ensure a positive buying experience for your customers.

1. Order Management:
    - Automated Order Processing: Implement automated order processing systems or use drop

shipping platforms to streamline order fulfillment. Automate order placement, tracking updates, and inventory management to reduce manual tasks and improve efficiency.

- Timely Order Fulfillment: Prioritize timely order fulfillment to meet customer expectations and minimize shipping delays. Communicate proactively with suppliers to ensure prompt processing and shipping of orders.

- Order Tracking and Updates:
  Provide customers with tracking
  information and order updates
  to keep them informed about the
  status of their purchases. Utilize
  tracking tools and integrations
  to monitor shipments and
  address any delivery issues
  promptly.

2. Customer Service:

   - Prompt Communication:
     Respond to customer inquiries
     and messages promptly to
     demonstrate responsiveness and

professionalism. Use eBay's messaging system or integrate with customer service tools to manage communication efficiently.

o Friendly and Helpful Support: Offer friendly and helpful customer support to assist customers with inquiries, issues, or returns. Provide clear instructions and solutions to resolve customer concerns and ensure a positive experience.

- o Resolution of Disputes: Handle

  disputes or issues with

  customers diplomatically and

  proactively. Work to resolve

  conflicts amicably, offer refunds

  or replacements when necessary,

  and escalate issues to eBay's

  resolution center if needed.

- o Feedback Management: Monitor

  and manage feedback from

  customers to maintain a positive

  seller reputation on eBay.

  Encourage satisfied customers

  to leave positive feedback and

address any negative feedback or concerns promptly and professionally.

3. Quality Control:

   o Product Quality Assurance: Ensure product quality and accuracy by conducting regular quality checks and inspections. Verify product specifications, packaging, and condition to maintain customer satisfaction and prevent returns or complaints.

- Supplier Performance Monitoring: Monitor supplier performance and reliability by tracking metrics such as order fulfillment times, product quality, and customer feedback. Address any issues or concerns with suppliers promptly to maintain a strong partnership.

4. Returns and Refunds:

- Clear Return Policies: Establish clear and transparent return policies to set customer expectations and facilitate hassle-free returns. Provide instructions for initiating returns and offer options for refunds, exchanges, or store credits.

- Efficient Returns Processing: Streamline returns processing and handle returns efficiently to minimize disruptions and maintain customer satisfaction. Communicate with customers throughout the returns process and process refunds promptly upon receipt of returned items.

5. Continuous Improvement:

- o Feedback Analysis: Analyze customer feedback, reviews, and ratings to identify areas for improvement and address recurring issues or concerns. Use feedback as valuable insights for refining products, services, and customer interactions.

- o Process Optimization: Continuously optimize order management and customer service processes to enhance efficiency and effectiveness. Implement feedback-driven improvements, automation, and training programs to enhance team performance and customer satisfaction.

By implementing these strategies for managing orders and providing exceptional customer service, you can build trust with your customers, increase satisfaction, and drive long-term success in your eBay drop shipping business. Prioritize efficiency, communication, and customer satisfaction to differentiate your business and thrive in a competitive marketplace.

Handling Orders Efficiently

Efficient order handling is crucial for maintaining customer satisfaction and running a successful eBay drop shipping business. Here are some tips to streamline the order handling process:

1. Automate Order Processing: Utilize automation tools and software to streamline order processing tasks such as order placement, tracking updates, and inventory management. Integrate

your eBay store with drop shipping platforms or order management systems to automate repetitive tasks and reduce manual workloads.

2. Set Clear Order Processing Times: Establish clear order processing times and communicate them to customers upfront. Clearly state your processing times in your product listings and shipping policies to manage customer expectations and avoid misunderstandings.

3. Prioritize Time-sensitive Orders: Prioritize time-sensitive orders, such

as expedited shipping or priority orders, to ensure prompt fulfillment. Implement workflows to identify and expedite urgent orders to meet customer deadlines and expectations.

4. Monitor Inventory Levels: Keep a close eye on inventory levels and stock availability to avoid overselling or out-of-stock situations. Set up automated inventory alerts or notifications to replenish stock levels proactively and prevent fulfillment delays.

5. Optimize Order Fulfillment Process: Streamline the order fulfillment process by optimizing workflows and minimizing manual steps. Organize your workspace, arrange products for easy access, and standardize packing procedures to improve efficiency and reduce errors.

6. Utilize Batch Processing: Batch process orders to optimize efficiency and save time. Group orders by criteria such as shipping method, product type, or destination to

streamline packing, labeling, and shipping processes.

7. Invest in Shipping Supplies: Invest in high-quality shipping supplies, such as packaging materials, labels, and packing tape, to ensure secure and professional packaging. Stock up on supplies in advance to avoid last-minute shortages and delays.

8. Track Shipments and Provide Updates: Monitor shipments closely and provide customers with timely tracking updates and delivery notifications. Utilize shipping carriers'

tracking tools or integrate with order management systems to track shipments and keep customers informed about their orders' status.

9. Implement Order Management Software: Consider investing in order management software or tools designed specifically for eBay sellers to streamline order processing, automate tasks, and centralize order management. Choose a solution that integrates seamlessly with eBay and offers features such as inventory

management, order tracking, and customer communication.

10.   Optimize Returns and Refunds Process: Establish clear and efficient processes for handling returns and refunds. Provide customers with clear instructions for initiating returns, streamline returns processing, and process refunds promptly upon receipt of returned items to maintain customer satisfaction and loyalty.

Prioritize communication, accuracy, and timeliness to build trust and loyalty with your customers and set your business up for long-term success.

Ensuring Timely Shipping and Delivery

Timely shipping and delivery are critical for providing a positive customer experience and maintaining satisfaction in your eBay drop shipping business. Here are some strategies to ensure timely shipping and delivery:

1. Set Realistic Handling Times: Establish realistic handling times for processing orders based on your

capacity and resources. Clearly

communicate handling times in your

product listings and shipping policies

to manage customer expectations.

2. Choose Reliable Suppliers: Partner

   with reliable suppliers who can fulfill

   orders promptly and consistently.

   Select suppliers with a track record of

   fast order processing and reliable

   shipping methods to minimize delays.

3. Monitor Supplier Performance:

   Monitor supplier performance closely

   and track metrics such as order

   processing times, shipping times, and

delivery reliability. Address any issues or delays with suppliers promptly to ensure timely fulfillment of orders.

4. Optimize Inventory Management: Implement efficient inventory management practices to ensure adequate stock levels and prevent out-of-stock situations. Utilize inventory management tools or software to track inventory levels in real-time and replenish stock proactively.

5. Utilize Fast Shipping Methods: Offer expedited shipping options such as

priority or express shipping to customers who require faster delivery. Partner with shipping carriers that offer reliable and expedited delivery services to meet customer deadlines.

6. Automate Order Fulfillment: Automate order fulfillment processes to streamline workflows and reduce processing times. Integrate your eBay store with order management systems or drop shipping platforms to automate order processing, tracking updates, and inventory management.

7. Utilize Drop Shipping Suppliers: Take advantage of drop shipping suppliers who offer fast and efficient order fulfillment services. Choose suppliers with warehouses located close to your target market to reduce shipping times and delivery costs.

8. Track Shipments: Monitor shipments closely and track packages using shipping carriers' tracking tools or order management systems. Provide customers with tracking information and updates to keep them informed about the status of their orders.

9. Communicate Delays Promptly: In the event of shipping delays or unforeseen circumstances, communicate with customers promptly and transparently. Notify customers about delays, provide explanations or updates, and offer solutions such as expedited shipping or refunds if necessary.

10. Optimize Packaging and Labeling: Streamline packaging and labeling processes to ensure orders are prepared for shipment quickly and accurately. Use standardized

packaging materials and labeling templates to expedite order processing and minimize errors.

11. Offer Order Consolidation: Consolidate orders whenever possible to reduce shipping costs and improve efficiency. Combine multiple items from the same supplier or warehouse into a single shipment to save on shipping expenses and expedite delivery.

Providing Exceptional Customer Support

Exceptional customer support is crucial for building trust, loyalty, and satisfaction among your eBay customers. Here are some strategies to provide outstanding customer support:

1. Prompt and Responsive Communication:

    o Respond to customer inquiries, messages, and concerns promptly and courteously. Aim to reply to messages within 24 hours or sooner to demonstrate responsiveness and professionalism.

- o Utilize eBay's messaging system or integrate with customer service tools to manage communication efficiently and ensure timely responses.

2. Clear and Detailed Product Information:

- o Provide clear and detailed product information in your listings to help customers make informed purchasing decisions. Include accurate product descriptions, specifications, dimensions, and photos to set clear expectations for customers.

- Anticipate common customer questions and address them preemptively in your listings to minimize inquiries and misunderstandings.

3. Personalized Assistance:

- Offer personalized assistance and support to address individual customer needs and concerns. Tailor your responses and recommendations based on each customer's preferences, requirements, and situation.

- o Build rapport with customers by addressing them by name, acknowledging their specific inquiries, and offering personalized solutions or recommendations.

4. Resolution of Issues and Complaints:

- o Handle customer issues and complaints promptly and professionally. Listen to customers' concerns attentively, empathize with their frustrations, and work to resolve issues satisfactorily.

- Offer solutions such as refunds, replacements, discounts, or store credits to resolve customer complaints and ensure their satisfaction. Apologize sincerely for any inconvenience caused and take ownership of the problem until it's resolved.

5. Transparency and Honesty:

- Be transparent and honest in your interactions with customers. Provide accurate

information about products,
pricing, shipping times, and
policies to build trust and
credibility.

o Disclose any limitations,
restrictions, or potential issues
with products upfront to manage
customer expectations and avoid
disappointments or
misunderstandings later on.

6. Proactive Communication:

o Proactively communicate with
customers throughout the
purchasing process to keep them

informed about their orders'
status, shipping updates, and
delivery timelines.

- o Send order confirmation emails,
  shipping notifications, and
  delivery updates to customers to
  reassure them that their orders
  are being processed and shipped
  promptly.

7. Follow-Up and Feedback Collection:

- o Follow up with customers after
  their orders have been delivered
  to ensure their satisfaction and
  gather feedback. Send

post-purchase emails or messages to solicit feedback, reviews, or testimonials from customers.

- o Use feedback to identify areas for improvement, address recurring issues, and refine your products or services to better meet customer needs and preferences.

8. Continuous Improvement:

- o Continuously evaluate and improve your customer support processes and practices based on

feedback, insights, and
performance metrics.

- ○ Invest in training and
  development for customer
  service representatives to
  enhance their communication
  skills, product knowledge, and
  problem-solving abilities.

Consistently delivering exceptional customer service will help you build a strong reputation, attract repeat business, and drive long-term success in your eBay drop shipping business.

Chapter 5: Optimizing and Scaling Your eBay Drop Shipping Business

In this final chapter, we explore strategies for optimizing and scaling your eBay drop shipping business to maximize efficiency, profitability, and growth. From refining your operations to expanding your product offerings, these tactics will help you take your business to the next level.

1. Streamline Operations:

    o Automate Routine Tasks: Implement automation tools and software to streamline repetitive tasks such as order processing, inventory management, and customer communication. Utilize eBay's APIs or third-party integrations to automate processes and save time.

○ Optimize Workflow: Analyze your business processes and identify areas for improvement. Streamline workflows, eliminate bottlenecks, and standardize procedures to increase efficiency and productivity.

- o Outsource Non-Core Functions:
  Consider outsourcing non-core
  functions such as customer
  service, accounting, or
  marketing to specialized service
  providers or virtual assistants.
  Outsourcing allows you to focus
  on core business activities and
  scale more effectively.

2. Expand Product Offerings:

  - o Diversify Product Portfolio:
    Expand your product offerings
    to appeal to a broader audience
    and capture new market

segments. Research trending products, niche markets, and complementary product categories to diversify your portfolio and attract more customers.

○ Source New Suppliers: Explore additional suppliers and wholesalers to access a wider range of products and secure competitive pricing. Expand your network of suppliers to mitigate risks and ensure a steady supply of inventory.

3. Optimize Pricing and Margins:

- Price Optimization:
  Continuously analyze pricing data, market trends, and competitor pricing to optimize your pricing strategy. Adjust prices dynamically based on demand, competition, and seasonality to maximize profitability while remaining competitive.

- Negotiate Better Terms: Negotiate better terms with suppliers to improve your profit margins. Seek volume discounts, favorable payment terms, or exclusive deals to reduce costs and increase profitability.

4. Invest in Marketing and Promotion:

   - Market Research: Conduct market research to identify target demographics, consumer preferences, and effective marketing channels. Understand your audience and tailor your marketing efforts to reach them effectively.

- Digital Marketing: Invest in digital marketing strategies such as search engine optimization (SEO), social media marketing, email marketing, and pay-per-click (PPC) advertising to increase visibility and drive traffic to your eBay listings.

- Promotions and Discounts: Offer promotions, discounts, or special deals to attract customers and encourage repeat purchases. Use eBay's promotional tools or create your own marketing campaigns to incentivize buying and boost sales.

5. Enhance Customer Experience:

    o   Improve Product Listings: Optimize your product listings with high-quality images, detailed descriptions, and persuasive copywriting to engage and inform potential buyers. Use eBay's listing optimization tools to improve visibility and search rankings.

- Provide Excellent Customer Service: Continue to prioritize exceptional customer service by addressing inquiries promptly, resolving issues efficiently, and exceeding customer expectations. Focus on building long-term relationships with customers to foster loyalty and repeat business.

6. Monitor Performance Metrics:

- Track Key Performance Indicators (KPIs): Monitor critical performance metrics such as sales volume, conversion rate, average order value, and customer satisfaction. Use eBay's seller dashboard or third-party analytics tools to track KPIs and assess business performance.

- Analyze Data and Trends: Analyze sales data, customer feedback, and market trends to identify patterns, opportunities, and areas for improvement. Use data-driven insights to make

informed decisions and optimize
business operations.

7. Plan for Scalability:

   o Scalable Infrastructure: Invest in
   scalable infrastructure, systems,
   and processes that can
   accommodate growth and
   expansion. Choose flexible
   solutions that can adapt to
   changing business needs and
   scale seamlessly as your
   business grows.

   o Prepare for Growth: Anticipate
   future growth and plan

accordingly by investing in resources, technology, and talent. Build a scalable business model that can support increased sales volume, expanded product lines, and additional market channels.

By implementing these strategies and continuously optimizing your eBay drop shipping business, you can achieve greater efficiency, profitability, and scalability. Stay agile, adapt to market changes, and remain customer-focused to thrive in the dynamic e-commerce landscape.

Implementing Effective Marketing Strategies

Effective marketing strategies are essential for driving traffic, increasing sales, and growing your eBay drop shipping business. Here are some strategies to implement:

1. Optimize eBay Listings:
   - Create compelling product listings with high-quality images, detailed descriptions, and relevant keywords to improve visibility and attract buyers.

- o Use eBay's listing optimization
    tools to optimize titles,
    descriptions, and item specifics
    for better search engine
    rankings.

2. Search Engine Optimization (SEO):

   - o Optimize your eBay store and
     listings for search engines to
     improve organic visibility.
     Incorporate relevant keywords,
     product attributes, and category
     tags into your listings.

   - o Use keyword research tools to
     identify high-volume,

low-competition keywords and incorporate them strategically into your listings.

3. Social Media Marketing:

   o Leverage social media platforms such as Facebook, Instagram, and Pinterest to promote your eBay listings and engage with potential customers.

   o Create visually appealing content, such as product photos, videos, and infographics, to showcase your products and attract attention.

- Engage with your audience by responding to comments, messages, and inquiries promptly. Run targeted ads and promotions to reach specific demographics and drive traffic to your eBay store.

4. Email Marketing:

   - Build an email list of subscribers and customers and send targeted email campaigns to promote your eBay listings, special offers, and promotions.

o Segment your email list based on customer preferences, purchase history, and behavior to deliver personalized and relevant content.

o Use email marketing automation tools to schedule campaigns, track performance metrics, and nurture customer relationships effectively.

5. Paid Advertising:

o Utilize paid advertising channels such as Google Ads, Bing Ads, and eBay Promoted Listings to

increase visibility and drive
targeted traffic to your listings.

- Set clear campaign objectives,
  target relevant keywords and
  demographics, and optimize ad
  creative and bidding strategies
  to maximize ROI.

- Monitor campaign performance,
  analyze metrics such as
  click-through rates and
  conversion rates, and adjust
  your advertising strategy
  accordingly.

6. Content Marketing:

    o Create valuable and informative
       content related to your products,
       industry, or niche to attract and
       engage your target audience.

    o Publish blog posts, articles,
       tutorials, or product reviews on
       your website or blog, and share
       them on social media to
       establish authority and build
       trust with potential customers.

- Collaborate with influencers, bloggers, or industry experts to create guest content or sponsored posts that promote your products to their audience.

7. Cross-Promotion and Partnerships:

    - Partner with complementary businesses, influencers, or bloggers to cross-promote each other's products and reach new audiences.

    - Collaborate on joint marketing campaigns, giveaways, or events to increase brand visibility,

credibility, and customer
acquisition.

- o Offer affiliate or referral
  programs to incentivize partners
  to promote your products and
  drive sales.

8. Customer Retention Strategies:

- o Implement customer retention
  strategies such as loyalty
  programs, exclusive discounts,
  and personalized
  recommendations to encourage
  repeat purchases and foster

long-term relationships with customers.

- o Collect feedback from customers, address their concerns promptly, and provide exceptional customer service to build loyalty and advocacy.

Monitoring Performance Metrics and Analytics

Monitoring performance metrics and analytics is crucial for evaluating the effectiveness of your marketing efforts, identifying areas for improvement, and making informed business decisions. Here are some key performance metrics and analytics to monitor for your eBay drop shipping business:

1. Sales Performance:
    - Monitor overall sales revenue, sales volume, and average order value (AOV) to track your business's financial performance.
    - Analyze sales trends over time, identify seasonal fluctuations, and compare performance against previous periods to assess growth and progress.

2. Conversion Rate:

  - Track conversion rates to measure the effectiveness of your marketing campaigns and product listings in converting visitors into buyers.

  - Calculate conversion rates for different traffic sources, such as organic search, paid advertising, and social media, to identify top-performing channels.

3. Traffic Sources:

  - Analyze traffic sources to understand where your website

visitors or eBay store visitors are coming from.

- o Monitor metrics such as referral traffic, search engine traffic, direct traffic, and social media traffic to identify high-performing channels and optimize your marketing efforts accordingly.

4. Customer Acquisition Cost (CAC):

- o Calculate the cost of acquiring each customer by dividing your total marketing expenses by the number of new customers acquired within a specific period.

- Monitor CAC to ensure that your marketing campaigns are generating a positive return on investment (ROI) and adjust your marketing budget and strategies accordingly.

5. Customer Lifetime Value (CLV):

- Determine the average lifetime value of your customers by analyzing their purchasing behavior, repeat purchase rates,

and average order value over
time.

- Monitor CLV to identify your most valuable customer segments, prioritize customer retention efforts, and allocate resources effectively to maximize long-term profitability.

6. Website and Listing Performance:

- Track website or eBay listing metrics such as page views, bounce rate, time on site, and click-through rate (CTR) to

assess user engagement and
effectiveness.

- Use website analytics tools like
  Google Analytics or eBay's seller
  dashboard to monitor
  performance metrics and
  identify opportunities for
  optimization.

7. Return on Investment (ROI):

- Calculate the return on
  investment for your marketing
  campaigns and initiatives by
  comparing the revenue

generated to the cost of investment.

- o Analyze ROI for different marketing channels, campaigns, or initiatives to identify the most effective strategies and allocate resources accordingly.

8. Customer Feedback and Reviews:

- o Monitor customer feedback, reviews, and ratings on eBay to gauge customer satisfaction and identify areas for improvement.
- o Pay attention to feedback trends, address negative reviews

promptly, and use positive feedback to showcase the quality of your products and services.

9. Competitor Analysis:

- Conduct competitive analysis to benchmark your performance against competitors and identify opportunities and threats in the market.

- Monitor competitors' pricing, product offerings, marketing strategies, and customer feedback to stay informed and

adapt your strategies
accordingly.

10.   A/B Testing:

o   Implement A/B testing or split
testing to experiment with
different marketing strategies,
messaging, or design elements
and measure their impact on
performance.

o   Test variables such as ad copy,
images, landing pages, or email
subject lines to optimize
conversion rates and improve
campaign effectiveness.

By monitoring these performance metrics and analytics regularly, you can gain valuable insights into your eBay drop shipping business's performance, identify areas for optimization, and make data-driven decisions to drive growth and success. Continuously iterate and refine your strategies based on insights from performance data to stay competitive and achieve your business goals.

Scaling Your Business for Long-Term Success

Scaling your eBay drop shipping business involves expanding operations, increasing revenue, and maximizing profitability while maintaining quality and efficiency. Here are some strategies to scale your business for long-term success:

1. Invest in Infrastructure:

    o Upgrade your infrastructure, systems, and technology to support increased sales volume and operational complexity. Invest in robust e-commerce platforms, order management systems, and automation tools to streamline processes and improve efficiency.

2. Expand Product Offerings:

- Diversify your product portfolio to appeal to a broader audience and capture new market segments. Continuously research and source new products, explore complementary product categories, and expand into trending niches to expand your customer base and increase sales opportunities.

3. Optimize Operations:

    o Streamline operations and

      optimize workflows to handle

      increased order volume

      efficiently. Standardize

      processes, implement

      automation, and leverage

      technology to reduce manual

      tasks, minimize errors, and

      improve productivity.

4. Scalable Logistics and Fulfillment:

    o Partner with reliable suppliers,

      shipping carriers, and

      fulfillment centers to scale your

logistics and fulfillment operations. Negotiate favorable terms, establish efficient shipping processes, and leverage technology to handle larger order volumes and meet customer demand.

5. Marketing and Promotion:

   - Increase investment in marketing and promotion to reach new audiences and drive sales growth. Expand your marketing channels, experiment with different strategies, and allocate resources to high-impact initiatives that deliver measurable results.

6. Customer Acquisition and Retention:

   o Focus on customer acquisition and retention strategies to sustain growth and build a loyal customer base. Implement targeted marketing campaigns, offer incentives for referrals or repeat purchases, and prioritize customer satisfaction to drive repeat business and increase customer lifetime value.

7. Financial Management:

   o Manage finances wisely and reinvest profits strategically to fuel growth and expansion. Allocate resources effectively, monitor cash flow, and maintain healthy profit margins to support scaling initiatives and ensure long-term sustainability.

8. Scale Responsibly:

   o Scale your business incrementally and responsibly to manage risks and avoid overextending resources. Set realistic growth targets, monitor performance metrics closely, and adjust strategies as needed to maintain profitability and stability while scaling operations.

9. Build a Strong Team:

   o As your business grows, invest in building a talented and dedicated team to support your operations and drive success. Hire skilled professionals, delegate responsibilities effectively, and foster a positive

company culture to attract and
retain top talent.

10. Continuous Improvement:

- Embrace a culture of continuous
  improvement and innovation to
  stay competitive and adapt to
  changing market dynamics.
  Solicit feedback from customers,
  employees, and stakeholders,
  and use insights to iterate on
  products, processes, and
  strategies to drive ongoing
  growth and success.

Conclusion

In conclusion, embarking on an eBay drop shipping venture in 2024 presents immense opportunities for aspiring entrepreneurs to tap into the lucrative world of e-commerce. Throughout this book, we have explored the fundamental concepts, strategies, and tactics necessary for beginners to navigate and succeed in the dynamic landscape of drop shipping on eBay.

We began by understanding the essence of drop shipping, its benefits, and why eBay serves as an ideal platform for beginners. We delved into the intricacies of setting up an eBay account, navigating policies, and conducting thorough product research to identify profitable niches and products.

Moving forward, we explored the practical aspects of finding reliable suppliers, evaluating product quality, and utilizing tools and platforms for effective product sourcing. We then transitioned into managing orders and customer service, emphasizing the importance of efficiency, communication, and customer satisfaction.

Furthermore, we discussed strategies for optimizing and scaling your eBay drop shipping business, from refining operations and expanding product offerings to enhancing marketing efforts and fostering long-term growth.

Ultimately, success in eBay drop shipping requires dedication, adaptability, and a commitment to continuous improvement. By applying the knowledge and strategies outlined in this book, beginners can lay a solid foundation for their eBay drop shipping journey and embark on a path towards long-term success in the competitive world of e-commerce.

As you embark on your eBay drop shipping journey, remember to stay informed, stay resilient, and embrace the opportunities and challenges that come your way. With perseverance and strategic execution, your eBay drop shipping business has the potential to thrive and flourish in the ever-evolving landscape of online retail.